The PRAYER PROJECT

By HEATHER SORENSON

To access INSTRUMENTAL and DEVOTIONAL PDFs, go to:
www.halleonard.com/mylibrary

2714-1353-1860-9956

ISBN 978-1-4950-6192-9

SHAWNEE PRESS

EXCLUSIVELY DISTRIBUTED BY

HAL•LEONARD®
CORPORATION
7777 W. BLUEMOUND RD. P.O. BOX 13819 MILWAUKEE, WI 53213

In Australia Contact:
Hal Leonard Australia Pty. Ltd.
4 Lentara Court
Cheltenham, Victoria, 3192 Australia
Email: ausadmin@halleonard.com.au

Visit Hal Leonard Online at
www.halleonard.com

Visit Shawnee Press Online at
www.shawneepress.com

Composer and arranger Heather Sorenson entered the church music industry in her twenties, and her name quickly became a welcomed fixture in the publishing world. Heather is hired by the largest and most respected publishers in the world, and her pieces remain at the top of bestseller lists.

Heather's publications include choral compositions, piano books, children's music, orchestrations and several albums. Her compositions are performed weekly in thousands of churches around the world, as well as in historic concert venues including the National Cathedral in Washington, D.C., DAR Constitution Hall, and Carnegie Hall.

Teaching has become a large part of Heather's career and ministry. She taught all elementary levels of music at Grace Academy of Dallas for 4 years, served as an adjunct music professor at Baylor University, and has served on many master class panels in piano and songwriting. Heather regularly is a guest speaker and conductor at churches across America, and leads scores of sessions each year at various worship conferences, schools and universities.

Currently Heather spends her time juggling a full writing load as well as traveling as a guest artist and lecturer. She makes her home in the Dallas, TX area with her beagle baby.

FOREWORD

I cry when I pray; God is listening to me. And so, when I was approached about doing a project on prayer, I immediately said, "yes." I'm not sure what my publisher had in mind when this album/book was first proposed, but I knew this was probably not going to be a "warm, fuzzy" project. I knew I was going to have to go deep. "So Be It" was especially difficult to write, as I was struggling at that time to reconcile my circumstances to the words that God was prompting me to write. When God wants me to pay special attention to what He is trying to tell me, He usually asks me to write a song about it. Funny how that works! I can look back on my repertoire and see lessons learned, tests I've yet to pass, and intense conversations with God.

As I immersed myself in *The Prayer Project* (we called it that for so long in production, that it eventually just became the official name), I struggled with prayer. It wasn't so much that I struggled with the act of praying—I struggled with the mystery of prayer. The summary of prayer goes beyond simply asking and receiving. Sometimes, we don't get what we expected, and at times, our prayers are met with seeming silence. Studying the broader scope of prayer in Scripture gives us a more complete picture; and yet still, there remains a mystery to prayer. You can find more of my thoughts on this topic in the downloadable content that goes with this book.

During my work on *The Prayer Project,* I carried some of my heaviest requests to God, and I wrestled deeply with this mystery of prayer. At the end of the project, my conclusion brought me back full circle to the first sentence of this foreword: "God is listening." Prayer is about the relationship. It's how I "draw near to God." He wants me to come to Him continually as I live my life. And, like a good Father, His response is always based on His love for me.

Praying without ceasing,

Heather

dedicated to the Praise Kids of Lavon Drive Baptist Church, Garland, Texas

THIS I PRAY

(Prayer for Others)

vocal solo, with opt. violin, cello, and synthesizer*

Words and Music by
HEATHER SORENSON (ASCAP)

* Parts for Violin, Cello, and Synthesizer available as a digital download
www.halleonard.com/mylibrary

mir - rored fa-cade,___ may you al - ways see your beau - ty through the

per - fect eyes of God.___ This I___ pray, this I___

pray, that you'd have God's_ best. Be strong___ and_ blessed. When your

arms are emp - ty, may your heart_ be full, ___ and the moun-tains that_ you face seem pos-si-ble._

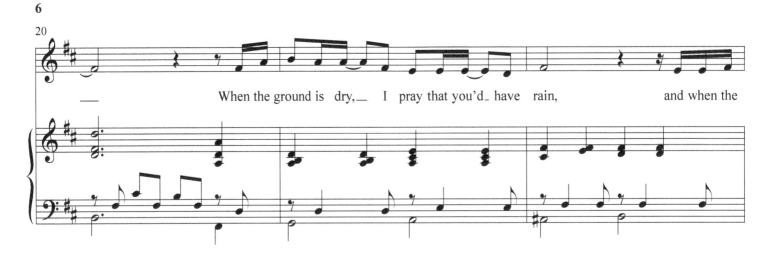

When the ground is dry,__ I pray that you'd__ have rain, and when the

mu - sic starts__ to van - ish,__ you would sing on__ through your pain.__ This I__

pray, this I__ pray, that you'd have God's__

best. Be strong__ and__ blessed. And when God's voice is si - lent, you'd hold

tight - er to___ His hand,___ and trust He'll lead you safe - ly on the

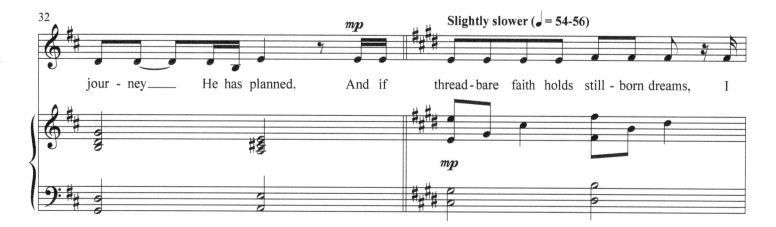

jour - ney___ He has planned. And if thread - bare faith holds still - born dreams, I

pray the hurt would be re - deemed. To hold on tight - ly to the Sav - ior,

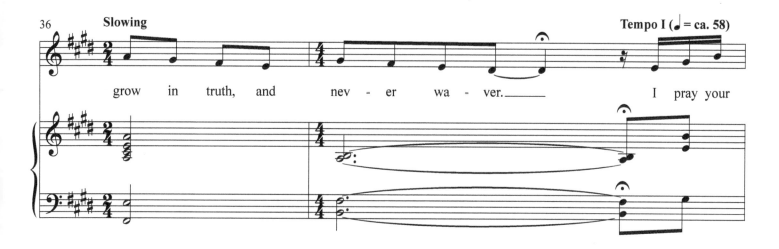

grow in truth, and nev - er wa - ver.___ I pray your

heart is warm___ when life can be___ so cold;___ and when

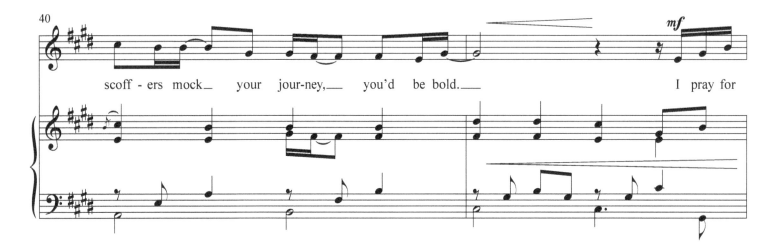

scoff - ers mock___ your jour-ney,___ you'd be bold.___ I pray for

food___ on___ your ta - ble___ in times___ when it's lean,___ and that you'd

share your meal___ with oth - ers so God's good-ness can be seen.___ This I___

pray, this I__ pray, this I__ pray, this I__

pray, that you'd have God's_ best. Be strong__ and_

blessed.___ That you'd have God's_ best. Be strong__ and_blessed.

UNTITLED
(Prayer of Worship)
piano solo

Music by
HEATHER SORENSON (ASCAP)

THE NEW LORD'S PRAYER

vocal solo, with opt. cello*

Words based on
Matthew 6:9-13

Music by
HEATHER SORENSON (ASCAP)

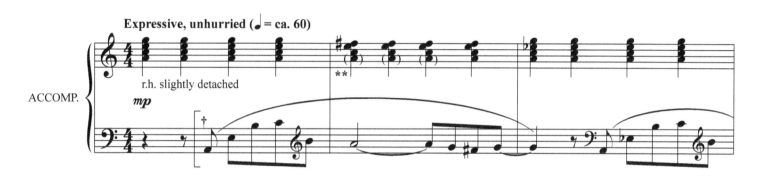

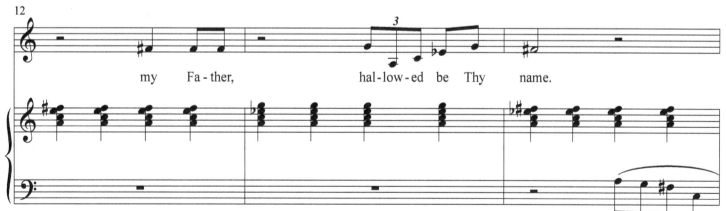

* Part for Cello available as a digital download
www.halleonard.com/mylibrary

** Do not play r.h. notes in ( ) when Cello is absent.

† Do not play notes in [ ] through m. 18 when Cello is present.

Thy king-dom come.___ Thy will be done,___ here on earth as it is in

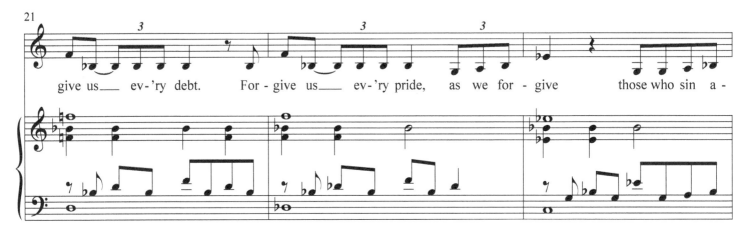

heav - en. Give us this day our dai - ly bread; and for -

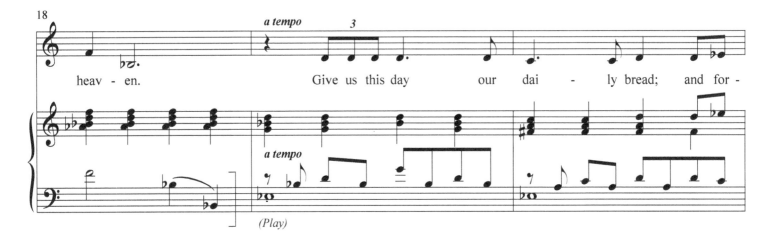

give us___ ev-'ry debt. For - give us___ ev-'ry pride, as we for - give those who sin a -

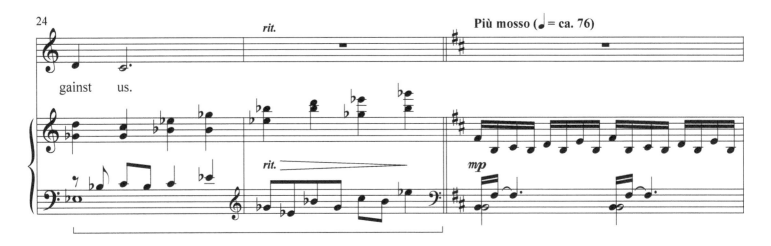

gainst us.

Lead us not in - to temp - ta - tion.

Lead us not in - to the e - vil. De -

liv - er us. De -

power,_____ the pow - er, and glo - ry for -

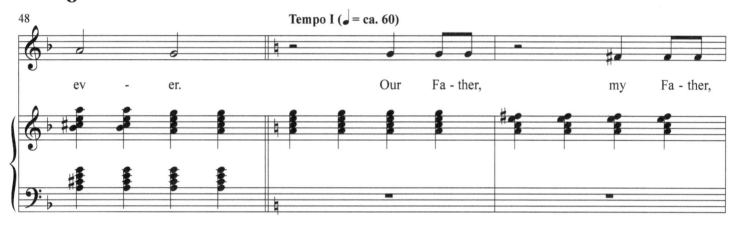

ev - er. Our Fa - ther, my Fa - ther,

hal-low-ed be Thy name. A - men.

A - men._____ A - men.____

SO BE IT

(If You Never)
(Prayer of Surrender)
vocal solo, with opt. violin and cello*

Words and Music by
HEATHER SORENSON (ASCAP)
Incorporating:
"'Tis So Sweet to Trust in Jesus"

* Parts for Violin and Cello available as a digital download
www.halleonard.com/mylibrary

never grow my dreams, but grow my faith in-stead,

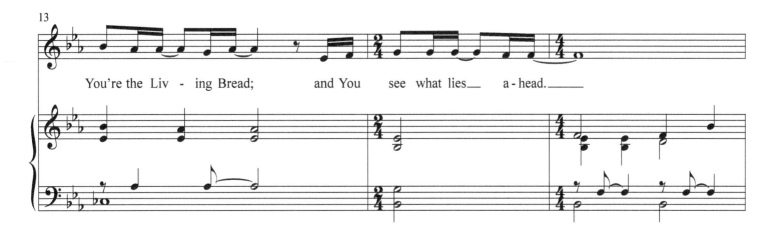

You're the Liv - ing Bread; and You see what lies a-head.

So be it. So be it, Lord. Lord, what You have in store

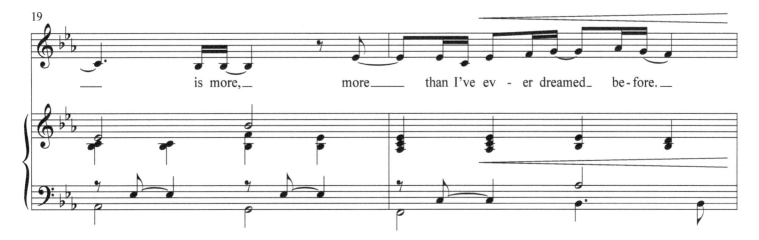

is more, more than I've ev - er dreamed be-fore.

So be it.___ So be it,___ Lord.___ Trade my will___ for

Yours. So lead me on___ the jour - ney You see fit.___ So

be it.___

If You nev - er do___ the mir - a - cle___ I

thought I'd see You do,___ if You nev - er feed___ five thou - sand with the

gifts I give___ to You,___ if the things I think___ I need will

keep my heart___ from know - ing the peace that comes___ from grow - ing___ in You,___

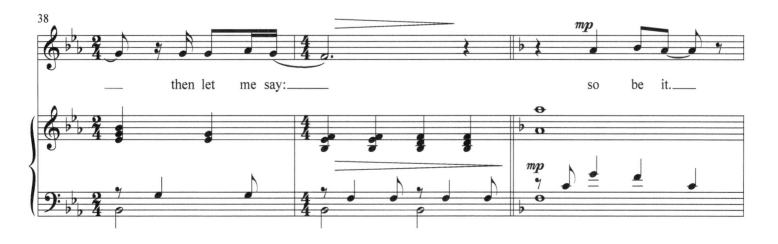

___ then let me say:_____ so be it.___

So be it,___ Lord.___ Lord, what You have in store___ is more,___ more

___ than I've ev - er dreamed_ be - fore._ So be it.___ So be it,___ Lord._

___ Trade my will_ for Yours. So lead me on_ the jour - ney You see fit._

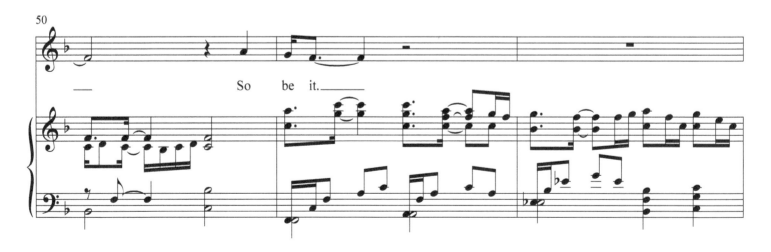

So be it._____

How I've proved You o - ver a - gain. Je - sus,___ Je - sus,

pre - cious Je - sus, oh, for grace, oh, for grace,___

oh, for grace to trust You___ more, trust You more!

So be it.___ So be it,___ Lord.___ Lord, what You have in store___

* Tune: TRUST IN JESUS, William J. Kirkpatrick, 1838-1921
  Words: Louisa M. R. Stead, 1850-1917

is more,__ more___ than I've ev - er dreamed_ be - fore.__ So be it.__

So be it,__ Lord.__ Trade my will__ for Yours. So

lead me on__ the jour - ney You see fit;__ and in the val - ley, teach_ me to sub-mit.__

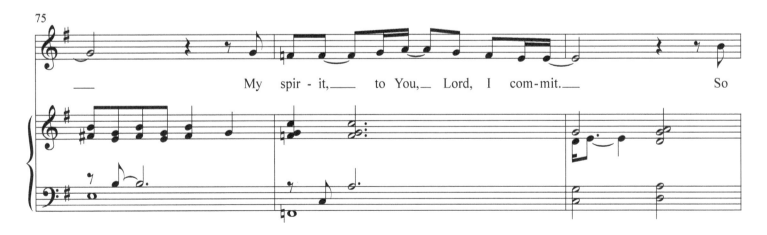

My spir - it,__ to You,__ Lord, I com-mit.__ So

be it._____

So be it._____

If You nev - er part__ the sea,__ then I'll walk with You__ on wa - ter. If You

nev - er light__ my path,__ then I'll walk at night__ with God._____

So be it._____

MORNING PRAYERS
(Prayer of New Beginnings)
piano solo

Music by
HEATHER SORENSON (ASCAP)

IN THIS HOUR

(Prayer of Restored Fellowship)

vocal solo, with opt. solo violin, solo cello, and strings*

Words and Music by
HEATHER SORENSON (ASCAP)

* Parts for Solo Violin, Solo Cello, and Strings (Violin 1&2, Cello, Double Bass) available as a digital download
www.halleonard.com/mylibrary

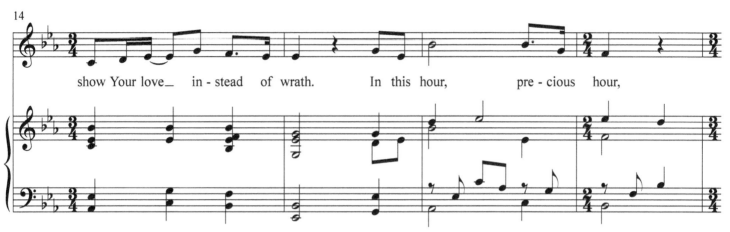

show Your love__ in-stead of wrath. In this hour, pre-cious hour,

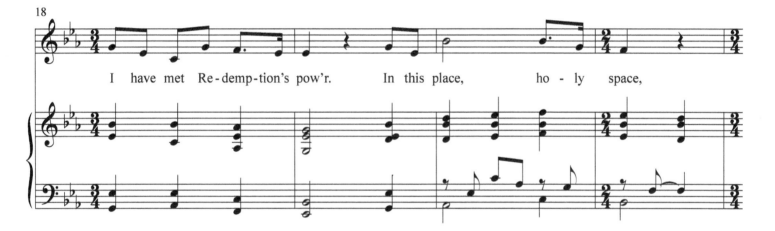

I have met Re-demp-tion's pow'r. In this place, ho-ly space,

I have seen__ a-maz-ing grace. Blis-tered soul__ be-gins to heal,

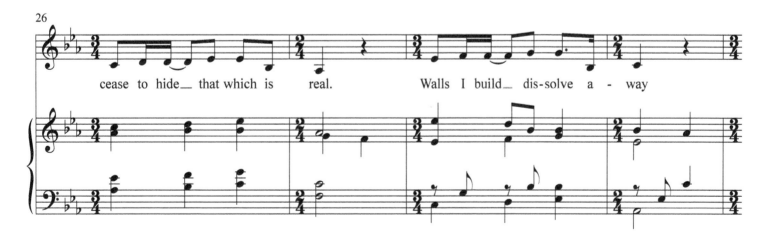

cease to hide__ that which is real. Walls I build__ dis-solve a-way

in this ho - ur when I pray. In this hour, pre - cious hour,

I have met Your heal - ing pow'r. In this place, ho - ly space,

I have seen__ a - maz - ing grace. Then gen - tle words__ be-tween us flow.

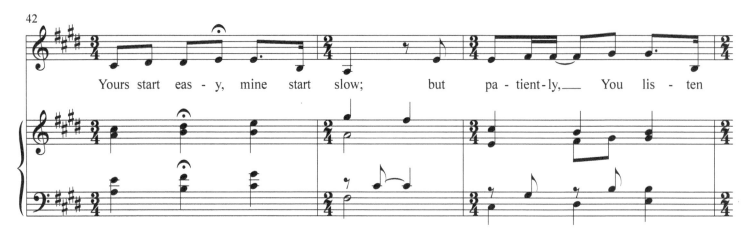

Yours start eas - y, mine start slow; but pa - tient-ly,__ You lis - ten

close to ev - 'ry bur - den I dis - close. In this

hour, pre - cious hour, I have met Com - pas - sion's pow'r. In this

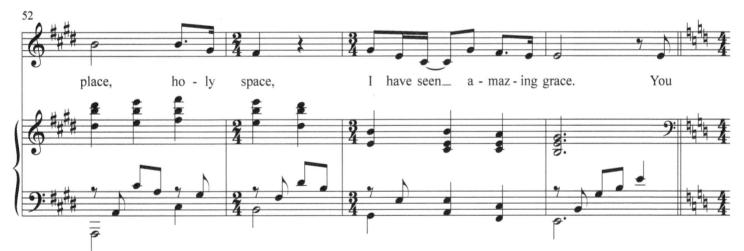

place, ho - ly space, I have seen___ a - maz - ing grace. You

help me with the words I can't yet say. And

when I can't quite reach You, You run to me half - way. And

if my heart is si - lent, You still stay in this

hour, when I pray. In

sea - sons of dis - tress and grief, my

* Tune: SWEET HOUR, William B. Bradbury, 1816-1868
Words: William W. Walford, 1772-1850

soul has of-ten___found re-lief._____ And

so You wait to meet me there, in this spe-cial place of

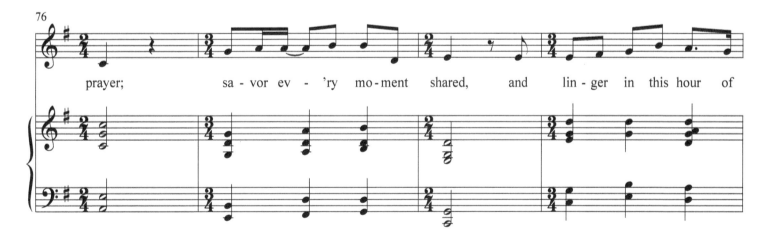

prayer; sa-vor ev - 'ry mo-ment shared, and lin-ger in this hour of

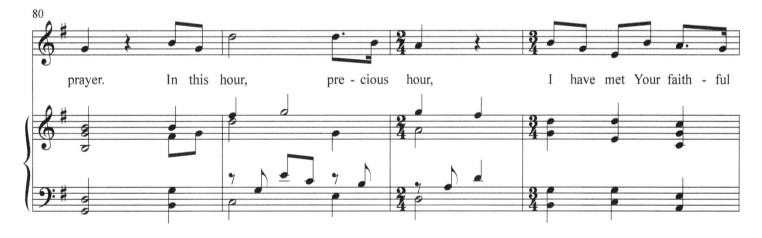

prayer. In this hour, pre-cious hour, I have met Your faith-ful

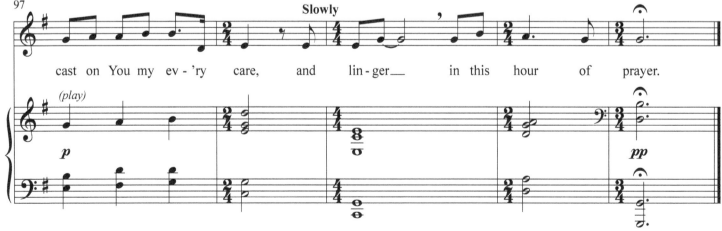

BE THOU MY VISION

(Prayer for Guidance)

piano solo

Tune: **SLANE**
Traditional Irish Melody
Arranged by
HEATHER SORENSON (ASCAP)

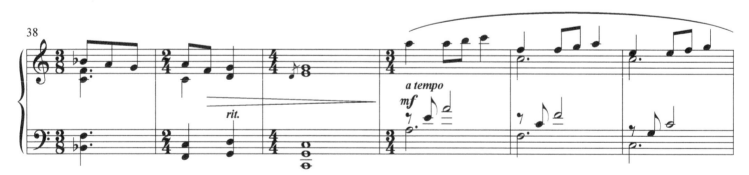

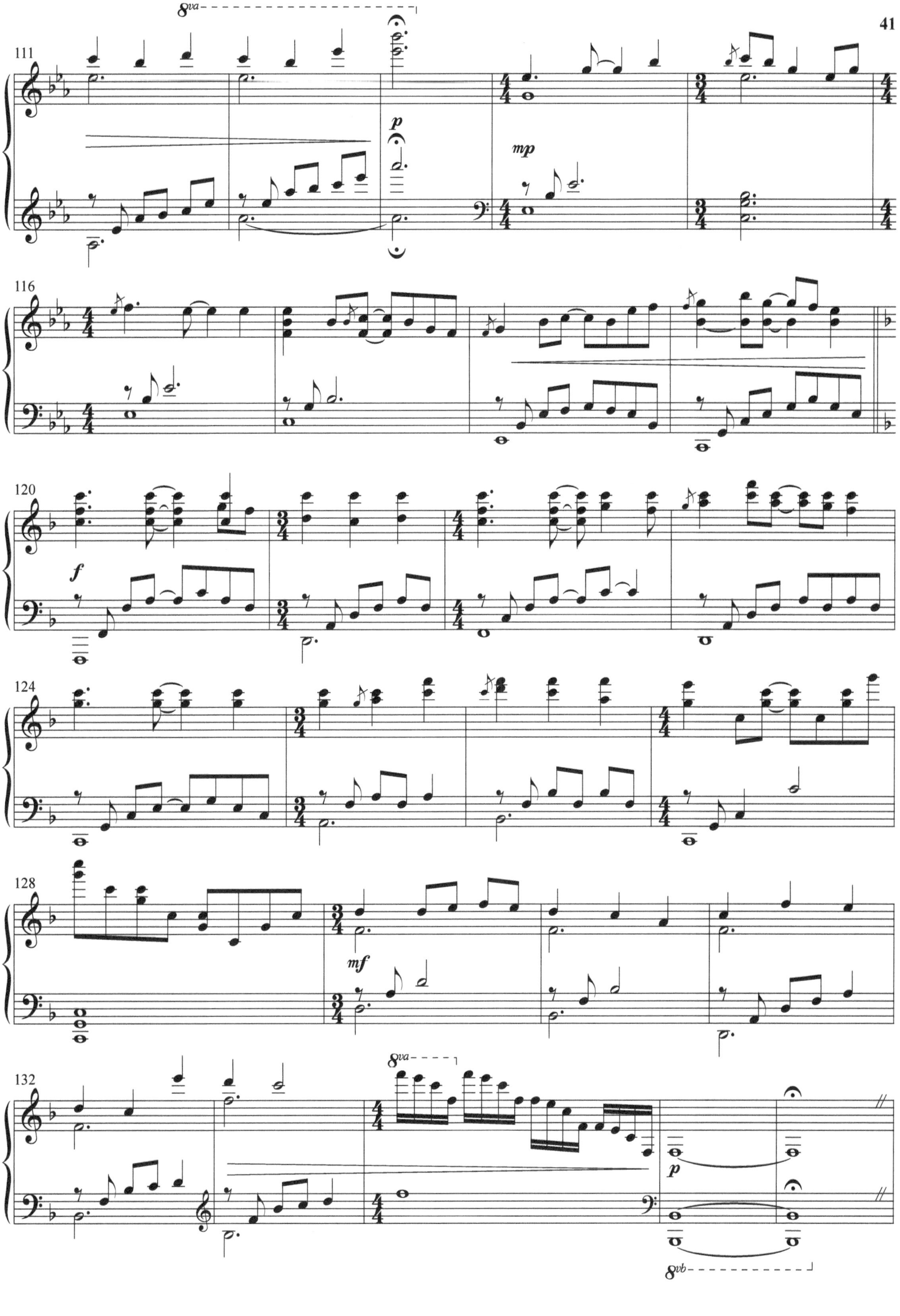
8va
111
p
mp
116
120
f
124
128
mf
132
8va
p
8vb

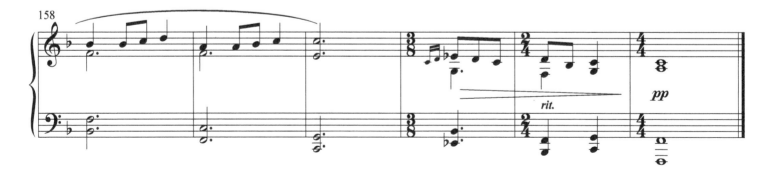

for Jachin Micah Johnston

LULLABY PRAYER

(Prayer for Children)

vocal solo (opt. duet), with opt. cello*

Words and Music by
HEATHER SORENSON (ASCAP)

Bless these lit - tle chil - dren, Lord; ti - ny souls, so a - dored. Lit - tle lambs to You be - long. They are weak. You are strong. When they're scared in dark of night, be their Light; hold them tight. Let them feel Your

* Part for Cello available as a digital download
www.halleonard.com/mylibrary

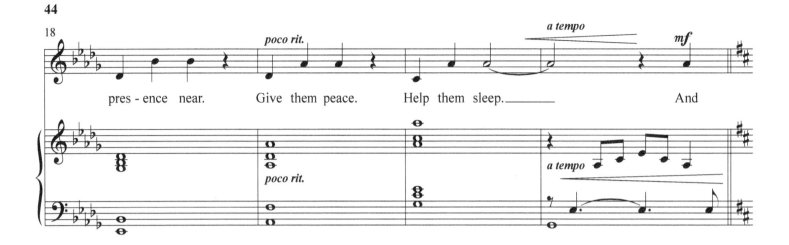

pres - ence near. Give them peace. Help them sleep._____ And

if their path goes through the cold, in Your arms, please en - fold.

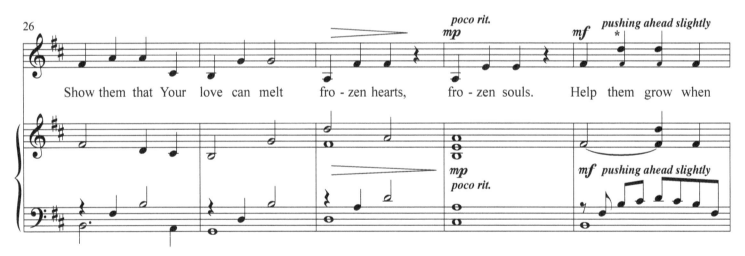

Show them that Your love can melt fro - zen hearts, fro - zen souls. Help them grow when

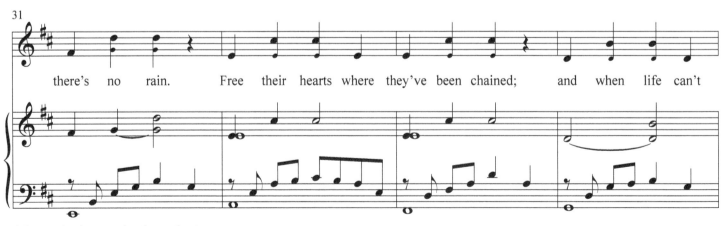

there's no rain. Free their hearts where they've been chained; and when life can't

* A second voice may sing the cued notes.

be ex-plained, oth-ers go, You re-main.

Give them faith for moun-tains tall. Guide them when faith is small.

Teach them how to fol-low You in their youth, walk in truth.

Help them to ac-cept Your love. Give them wings to rise a-bove the

noise that drowns out Your com-mands. Hold their hand. Help them stand.

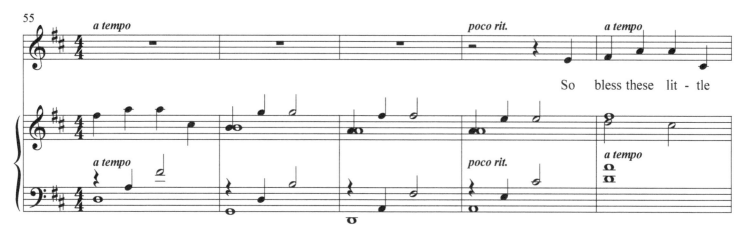

So bless these lit - tle

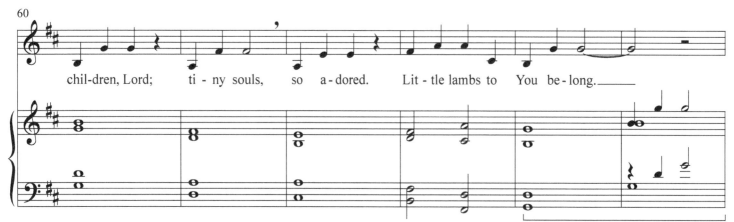

chil-dren, Lord; ti - ny souls, so a - dored. Lit - tle lambs to You be - long.___

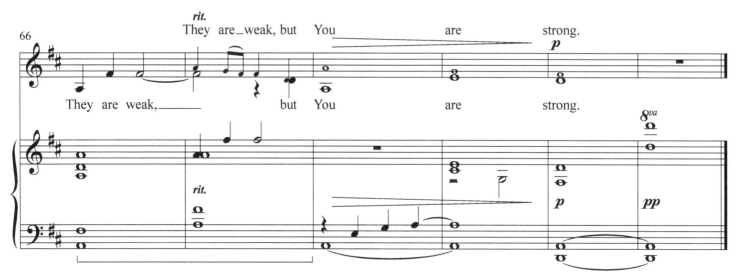

They are__weak, but You___ are strong.

They are weak,___ but You are strong.

AN EVENING PRAYER

(Prayer of Thankfulness)

piano solo, with opt. strings*

Music by
HEATHER SORENSON (ASCAP)

Molto rubato (♩ = ca. 88)

* Parts for Strings (Violin 1&2, Viola, Cello, Double Bass) available as a digital download
www.halleonard.com/mylibrary

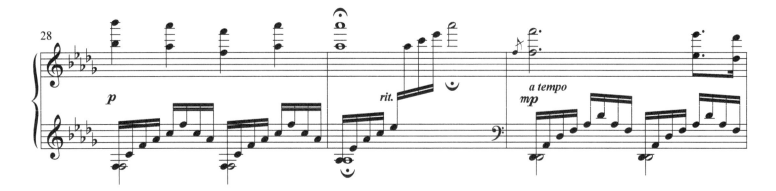

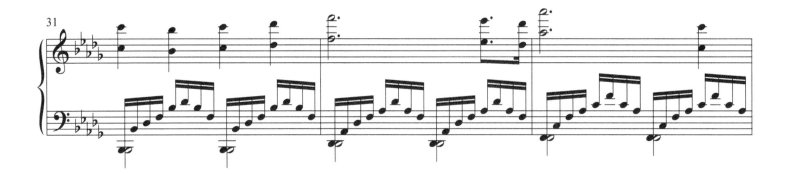

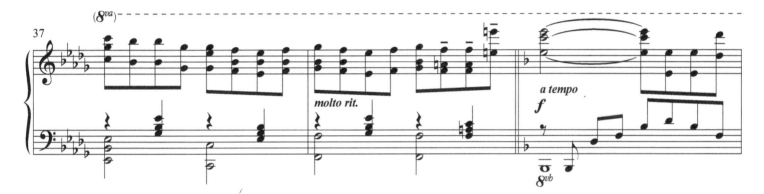

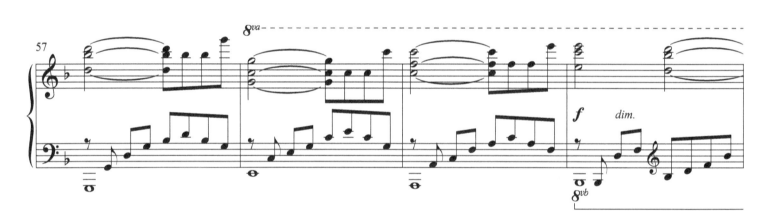

REMEMBRANCE
(Prayer of Remembering)
piano solo

Music by
HEATHER SORENSON (ASCAP)

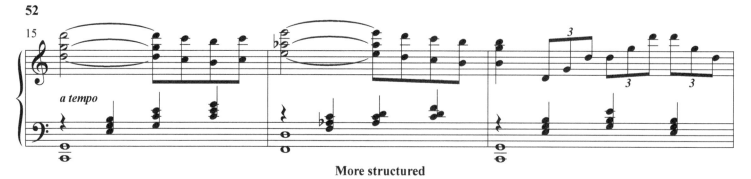

More structured

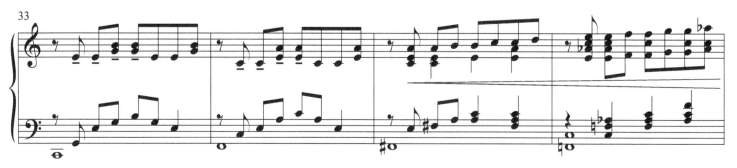

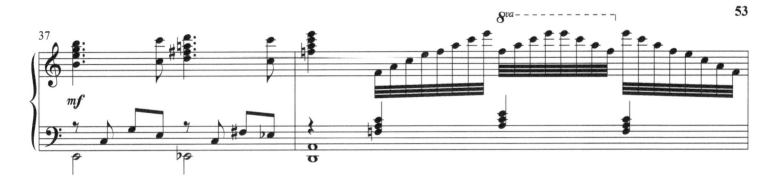

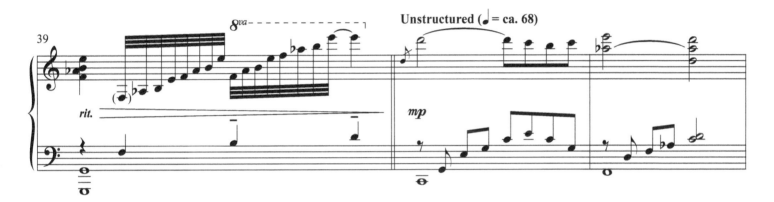

NEARER, MY GOD, TO THEE

(Prayer of Brokenness)
vocal solo

Words by
SARAH F. ADAMS (1805-1848)

Tune: **BETHANY**
by LOWELL MASON (1792-1872)
Additional Words and Music by
HEATHER SORENSON (ASCAP)

Near - er,___ my God, to Thee,___ near - er to___

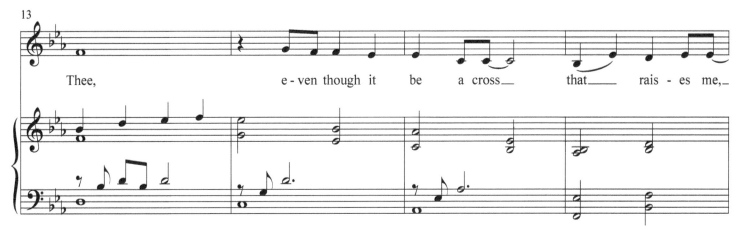

Thee, e - ven though it be a cross___ that___ rais - es me,___

___ that___ rais - es me.___ Still all my

prayer shall be,___ "Near - er, my God, to___ Thee."

Near - er,___ my God, to Thee,___ near - er, Lord, to Thee,___

near - er,___Lord, to Thee.__

And when the night - time hides Your face,_ dark is all__ I__

see. Then ur - gent-ly,__ my heart cries out,__

"Near - er, Lord,__ to__ Thee!" In Your pres - ence, I__ am

shel - tered. In Your pres - ence, I___ am___ strong. There is heal - ing for___ the

hurt - ing. There's for - give - ness for___ the___ wrong. You are hope for ev - 'ry

heart - ache. You are help for ev - 'ry___ need. Your a - bun - dant grace___ has

of - fered the prom - ise to___ be free._____

Near - er,— my God, to Thee,— near - er to— Thee,

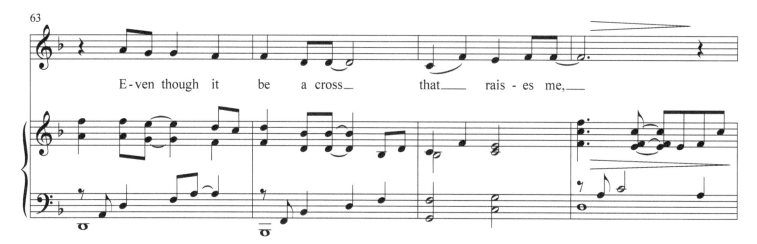

E - ven though it be a cross— that— rais - es me,—

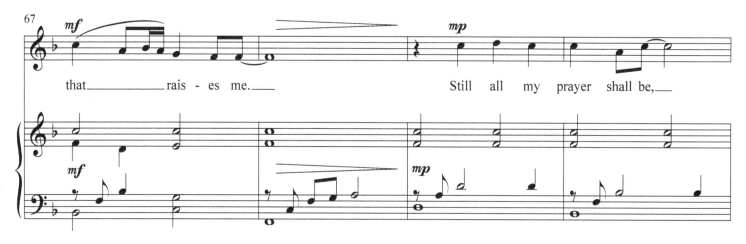

that— rais - es me.— Still all my prayer shall be,—

"Near - er, my God, to— Thee." Near - er,— my

God,   to Thee,___   near - er, Lord to Thee,___   near - er,___Lord, to Thee.._

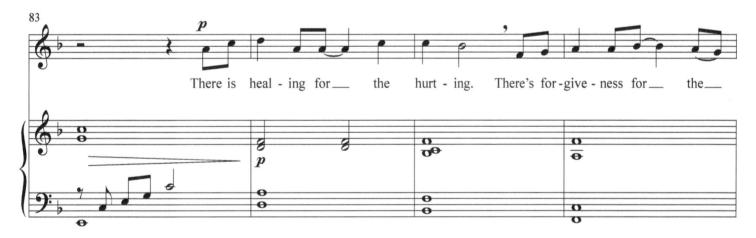

There is heal - ing for___ the hurt - ing. There's for -give -ness for___ the___

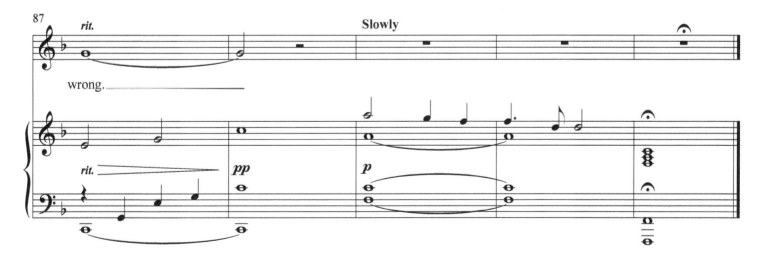

wrong._____